ONLINE WORD OF MOUTH

107 Blog Promotion Ideas for Creative Influencers Who Want to Grow Their Audience

DR. LIZ MUSIL

ISBN-10: 1539393356

ISBN-13: 978-1539393351

Poodle Mountain Publishing,

Rancho Palos Verdes, CA

Introduction

What is influencer marketing?

Influencer marketing relies on word of mouth recommendations. Thanks to social media, the power behind this style of marketing is vital to your brand and your blog. If you think about all the times you've asked a friend or family member for recommendations on restaurants, holiday destinations, or salons, you see how natural influencer marketing is. The reason you ask is that you trust their judgement, which is how influencer marketing works.

Finding relevant influencers is vital. There are influences within every market, the easiest way to find people is by seeking high engagement posts through hashtag searches. Promoting your blog is about being creative, making connections, and being consistent. It takes some time and persistence to gain an audience, grow a mailing list, and gain recognition. We all know the importance of building an email list. What's often overlooked is our overall impact – our sphere of influence. What is a sphere of influence? Your sphere of influence is your aggregate reach through all of your social media and marketing channels.

What is growth hacking? It's the process of experimenting across all marketing channels, and product development, in order to identify the most efficient and effective methods to grow a business. Growth hackers can be product managers, engineers and marketers that focus specifically on engaging users in an effort to build a business. It requires a combination of analytical thinking, creativity and social metrics.

As a blogger, you know how promotion can impact your overall success and get you in alignment with your goals. It is my hope the suggestions and ideas in this book will help you reach your dreams, whether they are to grow a following, sell products or services, or feel more confident in your marketing abilities.

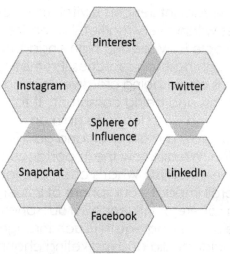

While researching this book, I learned that there weren't a lot of resources with strategic, actionable ideas to help creatives promote their blog. It is my hope that **Online Word of Mouth – 107 Blog Promotion Ideas** is a useful addition to your marketing toolkit. The suggestions in this book can be implemented in any order, and are meant to drive your inspiration and success to new horizons.

I wrote this book to help you get your products and services in front of the right audience. The strategies are not based on ideas or theory, but are tried and tested.

Wishing you an enjoyable, sparkly, sensational, and profitable journey.

Dr. Liz Musil

lizzietabitha.com

Use lead generating Twitter cards

Create a landing page

Create an email signature with a logo and link to your blog

Make your call-to-action prominently designed

Get interviewed in a Podcast, add your blog and landing page to the presentation notes

Discuss benefits for your audience

Share unique points about your company, product, and services

Enhance your interviews with stats, stories, and visuals

Mention bloggers and authors with large groups of followers in your posts

Tweet informative blog posts to influencers so they can promote them

Quote influencers in your posts, and let them know you promoted them

Ask others to share your content to widen your audience

Use Boardbooster to promote your Pinterest pins to group boards

*Create
professional
Pinterest boards,
Pinterest is an
evergreen site*

Host a Meetup on a relevant topic to your blog

Email your subscriber list when you post something new and ask for referrals

Include quotes from people your target audience admires

Recycle your content in various formats (blog post, Facebook post, links, images)

Create an online course and promote it

Promote the same content on social media in various formats

Share posts with LinkedIn groups

Develop relationships with people in your niche

Diversity your niche, widen your promotional circle

Share your influencers content regularly to build trust and goodwill

Have fun with your promotions: scavenger hunts, contests, etc.

Nurture your relationships

Co-create a product or service with an influencer

Host a joint Podcast or Webinar with an influencer

Comment on influencer blog posts

Send an email complementing a blogger on a post

Promote your blog on free promotion sites such as Stumbleupon and Bloglovin

Write epic, original content

Automate content pushes

Use graphics and statistics in your images and posts

Use hashtags to grow your audience

Experiment with paid advertising, such as Facebook ads

Find an active Pinterest group board to join using PinGroupie

Create a guest
post campaign
and open your
blog to other
authors

Optimize your blog posts using keywords

Ask for shares, comments, reposts

Link to other similar topic articles of influencers

Syndicate your blog post

Make video presentations of your blog posts and post to your YouTube channel

Ask an influencer for a quote to share

Turn content into a slide presentation and share on Slideshare

Convert your blog post into a .pdf file and share with social media groups

Pay to promote your content on Outbrain

Turn your content into a magazine on Flipboard

Publish quotes and snippets on Sulia

Use Google Alerts to find people posting similar content

Invest in some promotional swag – mugs, pencils, tote bags

Promote your blog on social media...

Facebook, Twitter, Instagram, Snapchat, Pinterest using a social sharing tools like SumoMe

Create a YouTube channel for your blog

Start a Podcast

Participate in charity work as an opportunity for networking

Host a contest or giveaway

Invite guest bloggers to post articles

Guest post on some online magazines

Publish an article on the Huffington Post

Invest in paid advertising

Create original images with text overlay

Be unique in your design and content

Be helpful in Facebook groups

Join online groups and participate in discussions

Understand the needs of your target market and create content to meet those needs

Reach out to influencers on Twitter

Add a downloadable pdf worksheet to each blog post

Promote each blog post with multiple images

Create an exit pop-up to catch visitors before they leave

Have several opt ins on your web pages

Announce a product launch and collect emails

Make your content easy to share with tools such as Click to Tweet

Publish more articles...aim for 16 or more a month

*Conduct expert
roundup
research
featuring other
influencers*

Create a resource article on a timely topic

Design visually appealing graphics

Interview owners of popular blogs and ask them to promote the post

Promote your blog on Quora.com

As various Podcasts to interview you...aim for one a month

*Create
soundbites of
your message to
Tweet*

Try advertising on Reddit

Join H.A.R.O, also known as Help a Reporter Out. A reporter may need your article

Join a blog support community

*Design your own
website and post
a link back in
your footer*

Post your awesome images to image sharing sites

Post a controversial response to an influencer post

Create a keyword research tactic

Ask an expert for advice

Promote other blogs you like in a post, then email the influencer

Promote your blog on Yelp, Google Business, Yahoo Local, Angie's List, BBB, Merchant Circle

Market your blog with AWeber and Buzzstream

Send a monthly newsletter to your email list and influencers you are building a relationship with

Schedule 10 - 15 Tweets of each blog post during the week

Share your blog post on Google Plus

Share your post with 5 Google Plus Communities

*Start your own
LinkedIn Group
to promote
others, then
yourself*

Pin your post to the top of your Twitter Page

Pin your post to the top of your Facebook Page

Place links in the middle of your Tweet

Mention an influencer in your post, then in your Tweet

Link out to at least 25 prominent bloggers in your niche

Submit your post to online magazines

Attach your latest blog post to your email signature with Wisestamp

Share your post on JustRetweet

Visit http://paper.li/n ewsstand and share your post on Paper.li

Host a networking event in your community

Research other influencers and publish a case study

Who is Dr. Liz Musil?

I'm a shadow ally to creatives, entrepreneurs, coaches, and teachers. I create actionable content to help anyone interested in growing a sustainable, profitable virtual enterprise. My videos, articles, eBooks and courses are about business, design, entrepreneurship, and technology. What is super-satisfying to me is achieving (and helping others achieve) self-reliance and financial independence.

An online entrepreneur since 2002, I work as a coach, consultant, designer, web developer, author, and professor. I teach entrepreneurship, leadership, and design at the university level and have completed research studies on virtual leadership.

I work out of my seaside villa located on a peninsula outside of Los Angeles, with my rescue dog, Zoe. Please visit at:

www.lizzietabitha.com

www.ingramcontent.com/pod-product-compliance
Lightning Source LLC
Chambersburg PA
CBHW071225050326
40689CB00011B/2464